**Articles
of War**

Marilyn Lengsteff

Articles
of War

Marilyn Longstaff

Smokestack Books
1 Lake Terrace, Grewelthorpe, Ripon HG4 3BU
e-mail: info@smokestack-books.co.uk
www.smokestack-books.co.uk

ISBN 978-0-9934547-6-9

Smokestack Books is
represented by Inpress Ltd

They were savage, single-minded, flying like battle machines

the women descending on Whitby from the cliff heights,
flying in the face of all opposition with their electric toothbrushes
that disturbed the peace of hearty walkers.

They would take no prisoners, these light battle maidens,
drowning their victims in vats of painted wool,
suffocating them in plaid dreams and denim.

They were on a literary trip and nothing would stop their flight
to better days before lycra.
There was no blood. This would be a bloodless coup –

involving stone hot-water bottles and warm vests;
there would be compulsory hats with wobbly bobbles
and definitely no stilettos –

fuelled by *Resolution* tea
and Botham's old-fashioned courtesy.

Contents

Bournemouth

It starts so well,
or else it starts badly,

unbelievably clear views
from the sea-front seen-better-days hotel,
or the force of rain bouncing up from the pavement.

Whichever it is,
there's always that mixture of hope
and disappointment:

if it's bad today, it can only get better,
if it's good, things can only get worse;

the counting of the days –
how long before we go back,
how long since we came –

the totalling of fine versus horrid,
balancing it up to see whether or not
we've had a good time.

Alioth Al-Jawn

The black horse John

Always beware the quiet ones my mother said
muttering something about hidden depths,
still waters and dark horses.

Unlike an Arab stallion, according to my Dad,
John had no rump; needed a belt
to hold his trousers up.

I couldn't say he raced into my life in 1968,

maybe trotted quietly, tossing his faintly curling mane –
long, with auburn lights; blinkered, myopic,
Mona Lisa smile.

My parents should have listened to their own advice.
While they were fantasising Christian weddings
with fiery Geoff or beaming Dave or sober Stuart,

the black horse, John, remained invisible,
galloped below their radar, nuzzled his dark way
into my affections.

Opposite Freedom Fields Park, 1961

My mother, in a fit of whimsy, locked us out,

decided we should walk, like tradesmen,
down the full length of the terrace – front,
then back – to enter through the yard
and scullery, keeping the new hall carpet
pristine, child-free.

One day, so tired from grammar school,
I camped out on the front step, with my bags,
my gabardine mack folded like a cushion;
I rang, then rapped, then howled and cried, then sat –
a battle of wills I'd never win.

The minutes then the hours passed. Eventually,
hungry, broken, cold, I had to give in.

After some months, she altered the regime –
forgot, couldn't be arsed – picked some other
weird and wonderful, meaningless power ritual.
I chose defiance, Frank kept quiet, then left,
Howard fled the country.

What did I learn?
       don't bother knocking
       find another way in
       power shifts
       there are no rules worth keeping.

Blue Books

On dedicating me to God, my parents
pledged to keep me from harmful reading.

My upbringing:
READ. MARK.

The Bible will provide everything you need,
The Believer's Bible – referenced for answers

to all problems.

Just the New Testament, mind,
and possibly the law and the prophets,

and a little smiting of enemies
in pursuit of salvation.

No sex and scandalous, adulterous kings
sending the cuckolded husband

into the front line of battle.

Although I did some illicit peeking, aged 13,
at the newly unbanned *Lady Chatterley's Lover*,

on the Canvey Island contract bus.
'A' level D.H. Lawrence's *Selected Essays*

proved the stumbling block,
which after much prayer, Dad permitted

for examination purposes.

This began the rot.
I still have a long way to go.

Articles of War

Hm,
> all that fuss

want   yearn   lust

diadem   gold   fur
> even a penguin can wear

though you must forswear

not just jewellery
but finery as well; beware

my girl, the path to hell

is paved with small steps
and you are taking them all,

> have taken them all.

What is prophesied will come to pass –
no crown in Glory for you.

> For you, a necklace
of concrete and broken glass.

Doll's Bonnet

Perfect in miniature.

Its crown, fabricated from plaited hat straw,
lacquered black,

spirals like an ammonite from centre
to rim.

Made by hatters who've plied this trade
for years

from Victorian high fashion to quaint
replica.

A fine tube of blood-red fabric
circles the brim

and maroon ribbon – three folds for Trinity –
emblazons

THE SALVATION ARMY
in gold.

And a deep navy silk ribboned bow, once tied
is fixed.

The chin strap shortened to fit her uniformed doll,
now lost,

like her Mum, whose proper bonnet
she keeps too,

like the ghost of the faith she's lost.

Headscarf

I have a traditional silk square scarf in pale blue, white and golds
that I took from my mother's drawers when I was house clearing.
I take it on most of my hillside walks (Mum hated walking),
a perfect companion in arctic conditions as light neck-warmer
and a Rita Tushingham head-cover, in strong sunshine.

I barely kept any of her clothes. We had different tastes
in colours and fabrics and style, plus she was much bigger.
But this silk scarf, not Mum's cup of tea,
a present from someone, I don't know who,
brings her closer to me, whenever I wear it.

Homeland

i.m. William Bramwell Crowhurst and East Grinstead
Salvation Army (closed 1967)

My little father was a 'man of Sussex', his town
East Grinstead and his ancestry quite static,
a line of labourers and domestic servants
all from the tiny triangle of Groombridge,

Ashurstwood and Forest Row. His mum,
my granny, once the daughter of a tanner,
became a champion of the poor, and now
she features in the town museum, clad

in her 'Army' uniform. Councillor, poet,
mother of eight children, she raised
her growing family in the ranks, and named
my father William Bramwell, for The Founder.

When Dad was called to service in God's Army,
to *storm the forts of darkness* down in Plymouth,
up to Darlington and all points in-between,
he left his home and made us rootless, scattered.

And we who sojourn in these northern uplands –
adopt its accent, marry out and change our names –
are branches of that family tree, the Finches,
Sargeants, Crowhursts and the Wellers.

We couldn't be more Sussex if we tried.

Torrent

after reading Philip Larkin's 'Water'

However angled light may be,
no glass of water would suffice
to capture faith for me;

perhaps for those brought up
in English Anglican ways,
of calm reflection and the nuances

that tolerate so many points of view.
Even the thought of *sousing*
in *a furious devout drench* requires

passivity, the notion of a shepherd god,
cleansing his flock with disinfectant
in a springtime rite.

The Yorkshire beck outside my window
captures more, running down steps
of unforgiving limestone bedrock.

On quiet days,
its dissembling trickle whispers past,
suggesting possibilities of safe crossing.

But overnight,
the gale-blown, fell-side rains
blast down this narrow gorge

and the stream rises, gushes,
roars.   They knew,
those non-conformist refugees,

who hid out in these upland fells,
that their jealous God
would thunder down the valleys,

crushing, flooding
everything in his wake.

THE LIFE IT SAVES COULD BE YOURS

after a photograph by Pat Maycroft of the life-belt at Sandsend

Here beside this notice we feel safe and clear,
our feet secure on the grassy verge, basking
in sunshine, whilst tampering mist creeps

over the sea to worm its insubstantial way
up Sandsend's valley, masking the village
and sharp cliff edges towards Kettleness.

It's coming though; whether today
or tomorrow. And the grass will turn brown
and wither, embrace its winter cover.

And the tide will ebb and flow, sometimes slow,
sometimes furious, battering sea defences
then sucking its booty into the depths.

That tiny couple on the water's edge,
will move with its rhythm, or die.
As must we all. Oh the bold confidence

of sign-writers and life-belt installers,
as if we have any power to save ourselves
or others.

Hairdressing

10 May 2011

This is my hair. Still cornfield blonde at almost 61.

Fine, flyaway, resistant to the cheap home perm
they tried when I was 4. And even though
I scratched out most of the offending irons,

a kink remained as evidenced in seaside snaps –
black and white sun-suit and my signature scowl.

Shoulder-length on our wedding day in 1971,

me in the midi dress I made and pale blue tights
and blue suede shoes. You with art college jeans,
a round-necked jumper and moustache, and cavalier

locks – we two against the adult world, in love,
convinced that if it didn't work, we'd get divorced.
Here we are still. Where have those 40 years gone?

As for my hair, its style today, it's down to Sean.

When I am young, say, somewhere in my twenties

I shall be thin again with no effort
eat peanut brittle, gorge on cinder toffee
go to The Plough every night at nine
and drink two pints of Newcastle Brown.

I'll wear tight green cords with button flies
and multicoloured stripy jumpers, have my hair
permed shoulder length, Pre-Raphaelite style,
stomp about in pink suede lace-up platforms.

I'll carry my heavy sun-bed to the pier end,
lie out in an unsuitably small bikini –
without sun screen – and when I fancy a break
have a plate of cockles and a Mr Whippy ice cream.

I'll learn to swear, and flirt with agnosticism,
go Greek Island hopping with two fellow travellers,
when I am thin again with no effort
and young – say, somewhere in my twenties.

And it stopped there

the bus, just 2 kilometres short of the unmissable temples;
so long ago she's struggling to recollect the place name.

So what to do, her flimsy dress, bought from a roadside bazaar,
moulded by sweat to her unsuitable body – the unattractiveness

of white perspiring skin?   There is no option but to walk,
We haven't come all this way, etc.

                                        And what can she recall
about these highly significant Buddhist stupas: well, the heat,

of course; the monks sporting unexpected digital watches
and slip-on shiny black shoes with gold chain detail; a group

of young men – surrounding her where she'd slumped on the grass,
while John went to admire the historic features – asking her hosts

of intimate questions. She draws attention to her otherwise occupied
spouse and the young men enquire if she has any children;

her negative reply, and theirs,
                    He has no power, your husband?

For the Triumph of Evil

You remember your parents
as good people, so when you hear them
parodied, infantilised, made quaint

by someone who should know better –
as part of clever over-dinner conversation,
the oyster and avocado pâté

sticks in your craw, and you are choking
to defend them, the words imprisoned
by a solid plug of indigestible food.

Later, in the privacy of your bedroom,
you want to shout, disturb the whole household,
redeem yourself, and them.

Saying Farewell Again

20 April 2013

that would have marked your 100th birthday,
I'm sending my hazy thoughts downstream
from my yellow-painted semi in West Crescent, Darlington,

from the Tees to the Itchen, Test, Avon, Bourne –
your distant southern rivers.
Barely a hint of bud in the lilac, after a long hard winter

as I say farewell again to you, lying as you wanted
close to The Solent, your Hampshire roots,
the sound of infants in the nearby school.

And I say fare thee well to my scattered siblings
as we share the 100th birthday
of our mitochondrial DNA.

Conversations

Tom is asleep in the all-embracing dirty-blue hospital chair-bed
provided for these occasions. He is worn out.
His seaside trip to visit his Grandma
has not turned out as expected.

Instead of the beach, a swim, fish and chips, a *Cornetto*,
he is trapped in the elderly stroke ward
next to his last living grandparent.
She is wired up and gently snoring.

I sit on a hard seat near to my mother's head,
breathe in, breathe out with her in unaccustomed silence
and rehearse all the conversations we never had,
never would've had, even if she'd lived.

View from the Delphi Hotel

white   shimmer of heat
orange/red gash of geraniums
a sapphire dome   the lapis sea

the now   the then   the time before

hierarchies change   religion
but it's still dog eat dog
the same old vision

It's the summer we'll never reach

This is the summer you'll
never reach, just beyond grasp
                    in memory's pit
excitement always at its edge

a state of neverendingness

A summer   untroubled
by winter's grip, that segues
           from eternal spring
forever days of hanging out

and short hot nights of glee

Where everything's before
you and **REGRET** is a word
you haven't learnt and even if
you had, you wouldn't

know its meaning.

Street in Samois

after the painting by Odilon Redon (1888)

Once, in this deserted street –

> a short street of golden stone
> that draws you in to its vanishing point;
> houses that conjure cosy, homely, warm,
> that promise interiors of workers,
> and their families eating, drinking,
> chatting at the kitchen table, houses
> that turn their backs on the outside silence –

Redon sketched a boy
carrying a heavy bundle of sticks,
weighed down in midday heat
labouring up the sandy road.

But now, as he and his wife
mourn the loss of their first child, Jean,
Redon removes the lad and his burden
from the final painting.

Wild Roses

Two girls in a cow parsley meadow;
the overblown hedges are full of rose blossom.

Two girls on the cusp, no longer quite children,
one putting roses in the long hair of the other.

It is heavy late summer, just before twilight,
the air thick with anticipation, and everything

about to be past its best. One girl puts roses
in the hair of the other, both look distressed.

Soon an unknown man will come to claim
the rose queen – he likes his meat fresh.

Fear of Waves

And if the Atlantic coast looks calm
I'll venture from the safer coves
on the Baie de Quiberon.

It isn't very far across this spit of land,
the flank of the isthmus,
from St Colomban, walkable to Ste Barbe.

But it's a world away
from swimming in the cold, flat, tiny bays,
to the risk of an ocean, uninterrupted to the USA.

So when the breakers come, which come
they will, I'm out of here,
I can't survive the swell.

Star-queller

When I lived in a house on the top of the moor
with more sky than land
more sky than home

more sky than sky could be,

and the almost constant mist
sank deep to the valley floor
or rose to the clouds

and the clouds were swept away,

I spent my nights in a room on the roof
or in the high branches of my one sycamore;
sometimes I lay on my back on a heather bed

star-gazing

light from heavenly bodies long since gone,
the patterns of stars, their geometric constellations,
wondering at their many man-made names;

in their dead light – star-bathing.

When I moved to a house with more trees and shrubs
and less sky than enough, I took up bird watching:
creatures of a more domestic sky,

alive in the now-light.

Sixth Sense

It was somewhere in the house.
She knew this sans doute.
And she had searched each room,
emptied every drawer and suitcase,
upended furniture, shaken down
curtains, but she was not sure
it would be visible if she did find it.

She thought it might be more to do
with a certain smell – no, not as strong –
a vague scent, an odour, a hint
of an essence of something very faint.
Yet that was not it either.

She tried turning both deaf aids
to full volume, scouring every cranny
but there was nothing except
the normal clicks and creaks of any
house after a hundred years of settling –
sounds she had not noticed since
her hearing started going, going, going.

So, she began to lick all surfaces,
run each taste around her palate.
Zilch.   Then she knew
she had no alternative but to store
all her worldly goods, and begin

dismantling.

That House

A house I'm glad we never owned
was the one at 19 Stockton Street,
so dull, the skeletons in the cupboard yawned.

I used to go there to play with Joan
my best friend. Fun, we made our own. We'd meet
at her house. I'm glad she never owned

anything interesting like a pedal-car or gramophone.
We'd fiddle for hours with an old doll, so neat
and dull. The skeletons in the cupboard yawned

at our endless games of hospitals, as we wound
her dead baby sister in an old sheet,
in Joan's house, the one I'm glad we never owned.

Where were her parents? Mine were at home,
glad that the child was out from under their feet,
a child so dull. In the cupboard, the skeletons moaned

as armies of police with shovels turned
the garden over to reveal the secrets
of that house.   I'm glad we never owned
that house where the skeletons in the cupboard mourn.

Not the Season

She sees he has cut the face from the October peach,
the place where he took a bite before it was ripe,
then sliced away the evidence of teeth, saliva,
and replaced it, damaged goods, in the bowl.

And time has sealed the scar, not much time,
a matter of days, enough to dry wet flesh,
grow a new smooth skin which puckers at the edge
where it joins the velvet cheek. His cast-off fruit

is ripened now and fit to eat, although has
lost its appeal, its youth, its succulence.

Fault Lines

After the first quake, I blotted you out,
dug deeper foundations,
was happier than I'd ever been,
put you in the bin,
closed the lid – it was a bin for shit.

Until you rattled the lid, broke free,
dancing like some manic marionette,
chanting the mantra
of your Mills & Boon puppet master,
shook me up again,

breathing fire and smoke,
smothering me in molten lava
that boiled the little pool I was basking in,
melting my resolve,
solidifying your intent.

Until I couldn't see my hands shaking
my limbs trembling.

Until all the china of my bones
was cracking,   shattering.

After the Disaster

After the flood, the mud,
after the mud, the devastated landscape,
the exclusion zone; the telephone lines were down,
there were no written communications;
everything had to be done through an interpreter.

After the bombshell, the fall out –
worse than the shock, the searing heat, the ash,
the nuclear winter. Time winds back,
replays, winds back, replays again:
the broken phone, the pulled out wires, the aftermath.

Fall

The sun will never shine this way again,
catching the glint of his intent, her confidence,
sending its heat at this particular time
after a long winter of discontent.

The light will never fall this way again,
illuminating their desire, chasing shadows
to a different scene, banishing the dark,
making them its children – wanton, blessed.

The breeze will never blow this way again,
tossing her August-cornfield hair, scattering
fears, rustling the leaves of once-young trees.
The night will never fall that way again.

Love Clichés

Back in the same room that an age ago
held you   *Obsession*, lingering
in the cushion folds, your nervous giggle
bothering my ear, the ghost of your look of horror
still-fixed in the over-mantle mirror
as your skin waxed greeny-grey,
your dark hair whitened.
And you shrank – in height and girth –
though you were very thin to start with.

You always said you were a coward,
but I, in that clichéd deafened-by-love way,
didn't hear   preferred to listen to
your honeyed darts, aimed straight
at the foolish ear in my heart, an ear
starved of the sound of sweet nothings.

Oh that it were nothing, or less
than nothing that you left behind.
Instead, you've tainted my room
with my idiocy.

Unsent

The yellow house is noticeable by its absence –
instead a massive roundabout.   Still there,
the house next door, a post-box in its wall.
I wonder, is this where he posted letters:

to Theo asking for a little money
for more paint, more canvas, perhaps some absinthe –
so he could make himself a nuisance
with the barmaid in the starry night café;

to Gauguin, offering a sunflower vision
of an artists' colony to rival Pont-Aven.
As soon as he arrived they argued.
He was never going to stay too long.

A clichéd tourist guidebook bit of fun,
to post my Van Gogh postcards here,
bar one. But underneath, a sadness –
lover – you notable by your long absence.

Don't you find

your friends: some opaque, some transparent?

Don't you find as you get older
    the grim reaper in a hoodie, looking into your window?

Don't you find as you get older you start seeing
    RIP on shop signs that once read *Lips*?

'Don't you find as you get older you start seeing through everything?'

Place Your Hand in the Wound

I'm in the Mission Hall again in Stalybridge,
'Come sister, just place your hand in the wound
of our risen Lord's side. Bring all your trouble
and lay it down at his feet. Only one step...'
Another hour of this – I check my watch.
Sweat on the minister's brow, tiny beads of silver,

washing away his sins. I need redemption. A silver
beam of light pierces the chapel gloom, a bridge
I run across, into the waking world, and watch
the strands of my parallel teen world wound
back in; wish I could find a way to sidestep
this haunting time-shift trap.   Trouble

always resurrects my nightmare. Real trouble,
like a mercury filling touched by silver
paper, only to be endured. He'll ask again. I step
into my husband's study. Glasses on the bridge
of his nose, he asks, 'Come with me,' (a wound
between us) 'to visit my dying sister.' Watch

your step, girl. Too late now, check your watch,
you don't want to go, too much trouble,
too many things to do before tomorrow, too wound
up, trot out excuses, tongue slippery as quicksilver.
My last resort, the usual quip, 'a bridge
too far'.   He's waiting on the doorstep.

I keep up the tirade as we step
out, just round the corner. I watch
him type the security code. We cross the bridge
into a world I don't want to see. Trouble
is waiting here, hiding its face behind silver-
haired women in wheelchairs, pop-socks wound

around ankles. I thrust my hand in the wound
of my mother's death bed. Only a step,
to the right path, or 30 pieces of silver.
Out from his wounded side – come sinner; watch
your heavy burden roll away, all your trouble –
rivers of mercy are flowing. Cross the bridge.

The nurse troubles to check her silver watch,
'Half an hour ago. I'm sorry.' I step across
death's bridge; place my hand in the wound.

Stag in Winter

for Isobel, after a photograph by Ian Short

Antlers held high, you stare
                stock still
                        through snow-mascara lashes
                                  at a point beyond the lens.

How can you disappear
                so seamlessly
                        and yet remain in view?

And how do you conjure the falling snow to be dun –
                            so that into it, you melt,
                                    as it melts into you?

All that betrays you
                is that red flash of another season's defiance
                                  on your thigh.

And the hunter feels your pride,
                sees you hold him in contempt,
                        knows you have a secret life beyond his shot;

although he may take your body,
                he can never tame your wild mind.

The Lickey Hills

So here you are in the back of the black car
(no idea what make).
It's October 1968.

A fresher, fresh from a puritan home,
scared stiff – of sin,
of consequences,   of your own nature.

What made you think you'd be safe
going to the pictures with a complete stranger,
even if he is 'of the faith'.

And you don't even fancy him.

Bad enough trying to shrug him off
all through the film (what was it?)
while the couple you went with,

the ones with the car,
(complete strangers too)
got down to some serious snogging.

But to get in the car after, in the pitch dark,

for a drive out to the Lickey Hills?
Well did you think they wanted
to admire the scenery?

And do you really believe that he
(whatever his name) is convinced
that you have x-ray vision –

so you can read the yachting magazine
you've found on the parcel shelf,
and feign an interest in Cowes Week

and boatyards and spinnakers?

City 69 – A Love Song

i)   The Station

First visited in waist-high snow, after the demise of Snow Hill
Railway Station, my train coming in like a young rutting stag;
windswept and half-lit tunnels where I did most of my
courting, apart from a brief disastrous encounter at Derby
Central. Was it ever sunlight? Was there a colour other than
concrete? Five Ways, Birmingham New Street, Decimalisation.

ii)   The Bedsit

In a white room with red carpet near the graveyard, rented
from Mr Pitt, the younger, we played *Disraeli Gears* to mask
the squeals from the communal bathroom. Breathy gas fire,
kitchenette corner with 50s blue Formica and the roar of
Corvette (Creda). Single bed, candlewick dressing gown, furry
slippers, woolly hat – and you one weekend in three.

iii)   *My Creda Corvette*

Most brilliant and economical of designs, harmonious in both
form and function, you obviate the need for kettles, boilers,
immersion heaters. With you, only you, I can have a hot wash
every morning, make pots of endless tea, wash up, and fill my
hot-water bottle. Your only restrictions: a rubber tube, a power
cut, and your eight pint capacity. I love you and your
high-pitched whine, whenever you're boiling.

Trip to Jerusalem

1969

I'm attractive
I don't sleep around
My boyfriend lives in another town

So although I'm flattered
by the way you look straight into my eyes and
excited when your fingers stroke my blue-stockinged shin
as we talk about student sit-ins and Led Zeppelin
and I like the sound of your name
Jim Crow
and the waves of your long black hair
you'll forgive me if I decline your invitation
to come back to your place for a coffee

I'll not be another notch on your one-night stand, baby
Just a ghost of a memory – maybe

Being Snogged by Elvis

No *Joy of Sex* in my childhood,
just Friday night Joy Hour at the Citadel –
Jesus first, **Y**ourself last and, in-between,
the **O**thers – the unruly and unwashed,
offspring from neighbouring terraces, singing
salvation choruses and watching flickering silent films.

My chuckling Dad, *The Kid*, transformed
from Captain/Major/Brigadier (*The Great Dictator*)
to projectionist – his favourite Chaplin moment:
Charlie's winsome puzzled look
as he boiled his gold-rush boots for sustenance,
testing the laces to see if they were done.

Commercial cinema was 'of the Devil'.
Once, off the leash at 14, visiting Margaret
in South Shields, we sneaked out to The Pictures,
Viva Las Vegas, the latest Elvis blockbuster,
and although my heart belonged to Lennon & McCartney,
a flicker of adulterous fantasy with the King.

Fast forward 40 years – lake-district panorama:
wet tree-less Keswick street in late November.
Husband-and-son-tied, I'm emerging from a pub
into the arms of a white-satin-suited, side-burned
slightly paunchy Elvis, and around the corner,
a stag do host of swaying others,

Mm Mm oh, oh, yeah, yeah.

Monosyllabic

Born at home in a mean street,
his Mum and Dad got a son too late,
the girls were grown but still at home –
two up, two down, so he had a bed
in his Mum and Dad's room.

No space of his own, lived
in his head, spoke when forced,
just plain *yes* or *no*, did not sing
in the choir, go to church high teas,
join in.   At school,

he found it hard to read and
do full stops. Failed tests.
He was a write-off.
But he could draw and paint,
was good at maths, liked facts;

Doc White saw a spark. And when
he got to sixth form, L.J. Bird,
who taught him art, said,
You are the best I've seen
come through these doors.

Swing Bridge Operator

I see him then,
              his look of disbelief

a quiet lad, monosyllabic, not the sharpest knife –
lived with his widowed mother – imprisoned
in this class of reprobates, all labelled

'less able', last lesson of eight
on a Thursday afternoon. And she,
not fully fledged, trying to teach RE.

They pushed and pushed and pushed
until she snapped, board rubber in her hand,
and clattered him, the only innocent.

Her uncontrollable tears, and the hardest girl,
with a hanky, put one arm around her shoulder,
'Don't cry Miss,' as she sobbed away her future.

John, let's call him that, was left, ignored
and bleeding. 'I'll tell my Mum
I tumbled down a bank.'

I see him over 40 years – flat cap,
boiler suit (faded), horn-rimmed glasses –
in the swing bridge booth, master of the bell,

grease for the cogs, a tide table.
              He never meets my eye.

Training to be a Zookeeper

'They're all animals,
as long as you remember that, you'll be OK.

Don't let them sniff your soft underbelly.
Beat the first one who steps out of line.

And never smile.' Advice
on the way to my first classroom from an old lag.

Just one snag,
I smiled as I took the class register:

> Jenny Bull
> Stuart Lamb
> Barbara Lyons
> Michael Swan....

A new RE teacher
thinking of Noah's Ark and Messianic order,

the sucking child playing on the hole of the asp,
and the weaned child putting his hand on the cockatrice' den,

had this odd notion that if I was fair,
interesting, kind,

they would invite me into their lair
as honorary friend.

RE Teachers

are almost always nice women on a mission,
who suffer, 'Swear ye not in front of the *God Squad*'
whenever they enter the staff room, and
'This is crap; don't want to be a nunstrokevicar'
somewhere in every lesson in the demountable i.e. hut
on the field; victims of the sadomasochistic humour
of senior management, who, if they know anything
at all, joke about Noah, and voices crying in the
wilderness; their worst enemies, the certain
maths teachers who know that they're important.

RE teachers are just about heartily sick of being content
with the crumbs from the rich man's table.

School Careers' Convention

for Liz

No chance of competing
with the electronic baby
as it set up its wail on cue,

worse than any burglar,
car, smoke or rape alarm,
its constant piercing racket

drowning out the Head
as she tried to welcome us all
to the Careers' Convention,

*Don't even think of having
a baby until you're at least 30,*
she concluded.

          I had the stand
next to the uncontrollable brat,
trying to engage a group

of 'interested in astro-physics'
students; just grabbed their
attention, when it was time

to change the electronic nappy.
What could be more enthralling
than that?

The Benefits of a Girls' High School Education

Mrs B was our atheist History teacher,
her Wednesday morning double lesson
70 minutes of clock-ticking hell,
'Open your *Eltons* girls, page 93' –
or sometimes it was *Mackies* –

'and read until the second bell.'

While she, her knitted twin-set breasts
sagging over the rim of the teacher's desk –
if she wore a bra you couldn't tell –
got on with her marking,
raising her eyes occasionally

above her half-moon glasses.

Barely a picture in the 976 pages.
Apart from the swots, we girls engaged
in a 'who can stay awake' competition,
turning unread pages
at intervals, regularly timed.

Not quite as bad as Friday afternoon

'A' level *Chaucer* in the medical room,
Miss Anon's soft tones in Middle English,
reading on and on and on.   Fiona,
her head back on the radiator, snoring,
and Margaret Wilson's loose-leaf file

falling from her sleeping lap.

Staff Do

The no-one-can-object-to music in the background,
my heart sinks in harmony with the low-level lighting.

'YOU SAID YOU WANTED SOMETHING CHEAP AND
CENTRAL.'

We jostle to sit next to someone we get on with,
the most polite, me, stuck near the dusty cheeseplant,

with Pauline.

A tired waiter brings the dated menu, and I ponder
which is the lesser evil, Minute Steak

or Cannelloni?

What do you fancy? Pauline asks. I know she needs me
to take charge – *I'm having cannelloni with an avocado*

fan and melon balls.

               I'll have same, she says and orders hers.

I'll have the fish, I say, wondering if they'll put a net
in the aquarium, *if it's not frozen.* It is. *OK, the steak*

not too well done.
                    It takes an age.

I hear myself asking, *How's your Mother, Pauline?*
and 'A GREAT NIGHT OUT,' from the other end of the table.

On (not) Hearing Simon Armitage
on *Start The Week*

April 2010

So it's come to this

the shower radio on at full blast
and I'm trying to make some sense
as I strain, sans mes appareils auditif
to hear what Simon says.

I recognise his flat vowels, the tone,
catch
   …'prose poems'…
   …'limestone crags'…
   …'domestic bliss'…
aware that I have never lived

within a three mile radius of the village
where I was born – the suburb of Mossley Hill,
Liverpool, in the *Salvation Army Mother and Baby Home* –
realise that, unlike him, I can never belong,

wonder, what else do I miss?

Terminus

after Temenos by Anish Kapoor, Middlesbrough

In January, my throat, thank God, gets the all clear,
so in February, the ENT computer decides to cancel
my annual audiology appointment.   And so I wait
in this light-poor overheated place, purgatory at the
arse-end of the NHS, for my records to disgorge
themselves from the hospital trust's bowels,

so I can sit in a windowless, sound-proof box,
netvast at its widemouth neck, straining to hear
the rushing wind, the fading beeps and whistles
that will chart my impending isolation from the
hearing world, when the only sounds will come
from the sacred space between my useless ears.

Hearing Aid Beige

Neither nowt nor summat.
Default safe. Never the colour

of joy, passion, rage.
A bull wouldn't give it

a second glance.
                              And yet

some idiot appliance-maker
thinks it blends into fair skin.

This is

the colour of disappointment,
the colour of fading sound.

Lost in Translation

LOST in muttering
O
S
T in thoughtlessness. LOST

In co
Ntext.   LOST in

Thought. LOST in whispe
Ring, LOST in
Accent, intonation. LOST in i
Ntellectual imperiali
Sm.
LOST in cultur
Al obfuscation. LOS
T in dialect. LOST. LOST
In the vacant
Open space betwee
N the saying and the heard.

Intensive Care

Around her bed:
the cochlea-damaged brother,

the otosclerosis sister-in-law.
And, inandout of her post-operative coma,

the deafened sister, lines going in and out
from every orifice and more.

Tragedy and comedy lie side by side
as she tries to speak and we try to hear –

could you repeat that, speak up a bit?
Of course she can't, so we employ

the well-learned strategies of the deaf:
me – the nonstop rambletriviachat;

he says nowt.
Six hearing aids between us

and none of them works well enough
to cope with the beeps and hums

and whooshes from banks of equipment,
the hushed tones of gravity, patient confidentiality.

She grips our hands as we try to offer support/comfort,
wishes that all will be well – and to stop her

pulling out the tubes.
She's irritated, confused.

On our way in and out we follow required ritual,
anoint our hands with some kind of antiseptic fluid.

At home, we'll wash until we bleed.

You watch us

with your ears tuned like a bat
in this house that has been deaf for years.

After you left, we got the flashing bell, with gong,
the one we take from room to room.

When you came back, I gave you 24 hours
before we jangled your nerves

though jet-lag made it 48. The subtle ways
you make us feel like strangers

in our own home – but it's the noise
that drives you mad,

your lack of comprehension that to us
it's all babble, a mutter, an irritating hum;

you indicate that even our noisy neighbours
have moved to use their distant sitting room.

Not to mention the way we
                    clatter pots,
                            slam doors,
snore.

BEWEARE BULL

Spelling the least of our worries,
as we are overtaken by fit cadets out on manoeuvres,
duck RAF trainer planes swooping down the valley, avoid
bog and newly formed lakes from months of downpours,
tractors with massive spikes, trundling, unheard behind us,
quad bikes zipping up rutted tracks,
rutting rams, heads down, in the lower pasture.

Then there is The Forgotten Map, The Forgotten Compass,
as we forget The Familiar Path and I insist we need
to be higher (note: lost here before) so, we mountaineer,
off-piste, scrabbling through broken-down dry stone walls,
crushed barbed wire fencing and knackered gates,
just before a 'shower' rewards us with a good drenching.
And my slippery-soled boots fall victim to glutinous mud,
tipping me into a heap of well-matured muck.

Surprising, really, we survive, those of us
who are old enough to know better,
make it for a pint in *The Green Dragon*,
reflect that there was no bull to be seen
anyweare.

Oriental Congress on the
Correct Use of Pinyin 1911

I don't know,

it's a bit like when someone misheard Kettering as catering;
I signed up for a course on the correct way of knitting

with size 11 needles, to be held in the oriental gallery,
side room, in East Cheam library

and found myself whisked off to this ORIENTAL CONGRESS in
Peking.
I have palled up with a very clever expert in the skill of pinyin.

Thank goodness I brought a variety of wool and a selection
of knitting needles. We are busy with a transliteration

of previously inaccessible-to-the-west
patterns for socks with one toe, birds' nests,

and huge cummerbunds, plus the Chinese emperor's tea cosy.
We intend to make a killing by publishing these in the new
Woman's Weekly.

First, I'm testing them out to make sure we get the right tension.
If all goes well, the expert is keen on transliteration/ translation

of English balaclava and vest patterns into Mandarin.

Elemental

He sucks in air, massive gulps, rinses it round his chest wall,
filters it through his lungs, breathes out fire,
red, gold, orange like his tangled mane,
napalms the rest of us with his dragon breath.

He paws the earth, his restless claws dig deep into its flesh,
his muscles twitch and pull with bottled rage,
he sucks in air, gargles it in his throat, opens his massive jaws,
and lion-roars the rest of us under a tsunami.

Graduation Photograph Arrives

I am back in my crisply contained feathered pit
and my wings are clipped, tied.

I did not expect to be back, and they
did not expect me.   Yet here

I am. My mother says,
'The photograph's good – it captures a rare smile.'

And I reply,
'I smile a lot when I'm happy. I'm just

not happy here.' Her face crumples.
I wish I'd lied – but she sees straight through me.

It's not that they're not kind,
that I don't love them, but

I'm not the boy that left,
and they are not those parents.

James Joyce's Mother Replies

No pen, no ink, no table, no room, no time, no quiet, no inclination

Shift off that bloody settee and get a grip.

No inclination, my arse;
you have been inclined, reclining
on that settee for three days and nights;

I'll give you *no room* – time, my son,
to find your own room, pay your own bills,
lounge about on your own furniture.

If I wanted a *table* in here, I'd have one.
I like to relax in my nice lounge,
watch a bit of TV,

instead of tripping over your long face,
and having to mop up the drips, nay pools
of Guinness that have flowed from your glass

every time you've dozed off.

I've bought you a packet of 10 HB pencils
and a notebook – now shove off
out of my sight. And keep your miserable thoughts

to yourself.

On the Impossibility of Producing a Venn Diagram of Human Emotion

Sounds easy, yeah –
just list emotions, his, then hers,
then circle where they coalesce.

They've been together years, so many years,
family and friends refer to them as one,
and she signs 'MAD' in texts
when contacting the kids (grown up, of course).

But think how many lives are run in parallel,
shouting across the tracks –
so what, we know that opposites attract

and now and then, when some controller moves the points,
their chassis almost touch and kiss,
then part again;
they're not apart, just not together, quite.

It's all straight lines and Venn requires
some curves, some give, some meeting
of the mind, the heart, the soul.

Maybe our couple have that in the ether,
in the feel of things,
something that can't be listed, quantified,
corralled.

For a Lost Love

The old girl has been tarted up so much
I fail to recognise her varicose lanes.
An operation has removed all clots
and she is neatly sewn into elastic skin.

Her once decaying rows of cottages are
crowned like teeth, they sparkle and gleam,
each in a pristine New England colour,
their smelly nooks and crannies sanitised,

lobster pots, nets and old trucks tidied away
in rustic sheds whilst car parks in her outskirts
spill their contents down her cliff paths in a wave
that laps up local ice cream and tourist tat.

My love, I miss your wild anarchic heart,
your shabby style, your strange vitality.

January

Lights. Lighter. The lights
in the office block over the road
go on a little later; TV flickering
in my new dentist's waiting room;
she'll decide whether or not my bottom right molar
is too shot to receive a crown,
after her last October root murder and
rubber-gloved November fiddling
with *spindly things* for root canals
in my propped frozen jaw;
'I really enjoy this,' she says.
Do I trust her? NO.
Maybe the beauty clinic next door,
which in the 1960s was a Calor Gas depot,
will get its drains fixed, offer me
a free make-over.

The Three Graces

after 'les trois baigneuses' by Henri Matisse (1907)

A hot beach, nowhere like Whitby,
china blue sea, turquoise sky.
And four bright white yachts
minding their own business.

Sweaty and pissed off,
three lasses have been swimming:
the arsey one, hand on her hip,
petulant mouth, high breasts,

no pubic hair, looks down
at the ginger-haired lass
crouching at her feet,
Stop snivelling,

NO, I'm not lending you
my towel, you should've
brought your own. Why
do I hang round with such

losers? The fat lass on the right,
hand over one ear, head bowed
in despair, sits on her heliotrope
towel, wishes she'd never come

knows it will always end in bother.

Second of Three

reflection on 'The Execution of Maximillian' 1867-8
by Edouard Manet (National Gallery)

The middle one

damaged
by damp
bad storage
the knife
neglect

Unlike the firstborn
eldest
heir
excitement of new
like first love

And not the youngest –
last chance for a baby

the one to be
nurtured
over-indulged –

but piggy in the middle

For a brief moment
the baby
a novelty
soon sloughed off
like an old skin
when the third one comes along

Thank God for the rescuers, the ones
who see only potential in this individual,
never make unfavourable comparisons.

Thank God for them, the savers
of fragments, the big picture restorers,
those who put the neglected

back in the frame.

Restoration Project

I had neglected the artist
let him fester
in his quiet studio
where spiders covered him
in cobwebs, and dust
inhabited the creases
of his socks.

The artist's hair grew greyer,
longer, curled in wisps above
his collar as he mouldered
at his easel, hovered around
his drawing board, surrounded
by all an artist's paraphernalia:
canvasses, fine brushes,
linseed oil, Rapidographs.

I'd renovated all the rest,
lavished attention
on the lesser lights
the insignificant.
So, it was time
to brush the artist down,

sandpaper his rough edges,
smooth with wire wool,
apply an undercoat
of brilliant white emulsion,
watch his eyes fade
behind whitened glasses,
hair solidify, hands fix,

then slosh on lovat green,
rub back, distress, wax, polish.
A little flesh peeps through,
a whisker, a hint of scruffy
Swaledale jumper.

Now, I've installed him
in the sitting room.

Naples

for Joanna

When I had the hysterectomy, my mother sent me
a get-well card with two fat babies on the front.
'Mother,' I said, shouting on the phone, 'Don't you think
that was a little insensitive?' When I got home, bleeding,
sore, stapled, sweaty, and made it to the living room sofa,
John had rented a video – Kenneth Branagh's *Frankenstein.*
'Enough said,' I thought.   My daughter Frances
is inter-railing by herself and I'm trying not to worry.
I'd helped her plan the route, persuaded her that Naples
wasn't the place for a seaside holiday. 'A bit rough
I've heard.' So, when I get the text saying, 'Naples is a bit
rough. Off to Pompeii tomorrow', I share my worry with my
best friend Joanna, who's had a few. 'Isn't Naples
a bit rough?' she observes. And being the sort of person
who tries to find a cultural or literary reference, decides
to add, 'Who was it who said, 'See Naples and die'?'

Alternative Ending

I disappeared, moved to the sea,
forged a new identity,

took up golf, enjoyed patience,
won back my hearing in a game of chance.

Then I found God, he wasn't lost,
just not quite where I'd left him off.

Finally, I caught a terminal disease,
its symptoms: happiness, contentment, ease.

Notes and acknowledgements

Dedication
The first line is taken from Douglas Adams, *Life, the Universe and Everything*.

Articles of War
Just as with the promises made at birth to keep me from harmful reading, my parents also vowed to keep me from jewellery and finery. When I was fourteen, I signed my Articles of War (to become a full soldier in The Salvation Army) which contained similar sorts of vows.

For the Triumph of Evil
This poem started from the last line ('you remember them as good people') from *When They Come for You* by Michael Swan.

It's the summer we'll never reach
This title is the first line of 'The Dance of Life' by John Burnside.

Fall
From an idea by Ann Graal (in response to a painting by Bonnard).

Love Clichés
The first line of this poem comes from a phrase found in a poetry workshop

Thanks are due to the editors of the following publications where some of these poems were first published – *Ink on Paper* (Mudfog, 2008), *The Eye of Temenos* (Ek Zuban, 2011), *When The Tramp Met The King* (Ek Zuban, 2013), *Going Gorgeous* (T-junction/mima, 2014), *Northbound* (Vane Women Press, 2016); *Arran News*, *Assent* magazine (Poetry Nottingham), *The Black Light Engine Room*, the Darlington Festival Literary Anthology 2014, the Hallgarth Summer School Anthology 2014 and East Grinstead Living magazine. 'Naples' was long-listed for the 2014 National Poetry Competition. Special thanks are due to S.J. Litherland for all her encouragement and astute help in putting this collection together.